W9-CEU-381

# THE
# UNEXPLAINED

# WE ARE
# NOT ALONE

Produced by Carlton Books Limited
20 Mortimer Street
London, W1N 7RD

Text and Design copyright © Carlton Books Limited 2001

First published in hardback edition in 2001 by Chelsea House Publishers, a subsidiary of
Haights Cross Communications. Printed and bound in Dubai.

First Printing
1 3 5 7 9 8 6 4 2

The Chelsea House World Wide Web address is http://www.chelseahouse.com

Library of Congress Cataloging-in-Publication Data applied for

Historic Realms of Marvels and Miracles  ISBN: 0-7910-6076-4
Ancient Worlds, Ancient Mysteries  ISBN: 0-7910-6077-2
Lost Worlds and Forgotten Secrets  ISBN: 0-7910-6078-0
We Are Not Alone  ISBN: 0-7910-6079-9
Imagining Other Worlds  ISBN: 0-7910-6080-2
Coming from the Skies  ISBN: 0-7910-6081-0
Making Contact  ISBN: 0-7910-6082-9

# THE UNEXPLAINED

# WE ARE NOT ALONE

## Searching the Heavens

Hilary Evans

Chelsea House Publishers

Philadelphia

# THE UNEXPLAINED

# WE ARE NOT ALONE

# CONTENTS

SUSCIPIT ERE MOSE (STORCA) XLMONS[...]E[...]TQU[...] AD[...]RE[...] RDOCE XHPOPULO REPLETUS NECTARE SCO V

# Imagining Other Worlds

**And the Lord said unto Moses, "Lo, I come unto thee in a thick cloud, that the people may hear when I speak with thee, and believe thee for ever". And Moses brought forth the people to meet with God; and Mount Sinai was altogether on a smoke, because the Lord descended upon it in fire, and the whole mount quaked greatly. And when Moses spake, God answered him by a voice … And all the people saw the thunderings, and the lightnings, and the mountain smoking: and they said unto Moses, "Let not God speak with us, lest we die."**

**… Then went up Moses, and seventy of the elders; and they saw the God of Israel; and there was under his feet as it were a paved work of sapphire stone. Upon the nobles of the children of Israel he laid not his hand: also they saw God… and he gave unto Moses two tables of stone, written with the finger of God …**

Earth's first visitors from other worlds were gods. This was when mankind was still a new idea: those who had created us wanted to know how we were getting on, make sure we were behaving ourselves. So they came to see us with their own eyes.

The most famous of all meetings between Man and his creator is the encounter of Moses with the God of Israel on Mount Sinai, when God gives Moses instructions as to what the people of Israel should do and should not do, promising them rewards if they do as he tells them, punishments if they don't. He is an all-powerful god, yet he takes note of what his creatures say, and unlike most absolute rulers, his mind can be swayed. Angry when the people of Israel go whoring after strange gods, he tells Moses, "I have seen this people, and behold, it is a stiff-necked people: now therefore leave me alone, that my wrath may wax hot against them, and that I may consume them." But he listens when Moses speaks up in their defence, "and the Lord repented of the evil

*LEFT: An illuminated manuscript (c.840) depicting God giving Moses the Tables of the Law on Mount Sinai.*

which he thought to do unto his people".

So Moses makes a covenant with God, and God presents him with a set of the Ten Commandments: "And the tables were the work of God, and the writing was the writing of God, graven upon the tables".

Although Moses, along with his senior colleagues, is described as seeing God, he has not really seen him face to face. When he asks "I beseech thee, show me thy glory", God answers "Thou canst not see my face; for there shall no man see me, and live". But he considerately adds, "Behold, I will put thee in a clift of the rock, and will cover thee with my hand while I pass by; and I will take away mine hand, and thou shalt see my back parts; but my face shall not be seen".

We cannot know when, how, or why man raised his head from the concerns of his everyday life to contemplate higher levels of reality. But it seems there was never a time when man did not feel that otherworldly realms existed. Our earliest records show an awareness of superior, superhuman beings, who from time to time made their presence known to the inhabitants of Earth.

Why should our ancestors, who we would expect to be preoccupied with surviving the risks of life on Earth and dealing with the complexities of living with their fellow humans, bother with the Heavens which, to all appearances, are remote and irrelevant to their existence? Some philosophers hold that a propensity for religious belief is inherent in the human state, that it is one of the things that makes us human. Perhaps even the caveman, along with the instinct for survival he shared with the bears and tigers, had something more, this sense of the numinous. Alternatively, maybe it was simply a more highly-developed version of the pecking order between animals, or the respect a dog has for its master. Or was it the first stirrings of scientific curiosity, driving people to speculate as to the origin of thunder and lightning and consider where they themselves came from, leading them to the reasonable conclusion that there must be gods?

On the other hand, could the ancient chronicles record fact, not fable? Did our earliest ancestors believe in gods because they actually met them, face to face? There can be no doubt that, so far as the author of the book of Exodus was

*Ramses IV with the god Horus : the Egyptians depicted their rulers enjoying actual meetings with divine beings.*

otherworldly beings described in this book, and if not, where do we propose to draw a line?

These questions will confront us throughout this survey. Whether we are concerned with gods or demons, spirits of the dead or extraterrestrial aliens, we shall find ourselves in the same dilemma – are these stories of visits and encounters with otherworldly beings based on real experiences, or are they no more than wishful or fearful thinking? Do the beings themselves physically exist, or are they simply fanciful inventions, saviours or bogeymen created by ourselves as outward embodiments of our hopes, fears and expectations?

Even if we conclude that the stories the Greeks told about Zeus and Athena – or that the Egyptians told about Horus, or the Norse about Thor – are no more than legends, we may still ask if the remote origins of those legends were rooted in fact. Did real beings do real things which were magnified into tales of superhuman gods? That encounters with beings from other worlds have indeed taken place is often not easy to believe, to say the least. Equally however, it is hard to believe that stories so widespread and so persistent are nothing more than out-and-out fantasy. When we come to our own day, we shall see that man has lost none of his ability to create elaborate myths out of simple happenings. Statues that weep or drink milk, phone calls from the dead, aliens who beam us up through the air to their hovering spacecraft – man's ability to believe in wonders never ceases. Should we see this mythmaking skill as a childhood phase we ought to have grown out of by now, or as one of the most enduring, and endearing, of man's attributes?

It is easy for educated citizens of advanced cultures to relegate such stories as God's meeting with Moses to the category of myth and legend. But a blanket dismissal of this kind hides the fact that what we see as myth was, for millions of people – many of them thoughtful and intelligent – a powerful reality. The Crusaders who went to war in the name of the Christian god and the Saracens who resisted them in the name of Allah were not all cynics and pious frauds. Many, perhaps most, devoutly

concerned, Moses had been privileged to have a physical encounter with the God of Israel. This is no metaphor, no pious abstraction: He spoke, He wrote, He became angry, He changed His mind. And Moses had seen His back parts, at least, and if God had not allowed him to see His face, it was for his own good, for He knew that no-one could do so and live to tell the tale.

Few who read this book will be prepared to say that yes, they believe that Moses did actually meet God, or that the Greek warriors who besieged Troy enjoyed the daily interaction with their gods and goddesses that Homer describes. But are we prepared to assert that these things are total fabrication? If so, will we be equally sceptical with all the other claims of encounter with believed they were carrying out their god's will. Nor is it only the Supreme Deity who commands genuine belief. A few years ago I attended a prestigious conference in Basel, where an Austrian professor presented a paper on the phenomenon known as diabolical possession. I took it for granted that as a highly educated person he would regard the phenomenon as, at best, a psychological delusion. Not a bit of it: to my astonishment I learnt that he firmly believed his subject had been possessed by an evil spirit as actual and material as any described in medieval legend.

# OTHER LEVELS OF REALITY

Many of the stories of visits from other worlds defy our sense of what is "real". The Virgin Mary visits Bernadette Soubirous at Lourdes, where she is seen by Bernadette but not by those standing right beside her. Joseph Smith is visited by an angel who reveals to him the Book of Mormon, but no one else sees either the angel or the golden pages. Linda Napolitano is visited by aliens who carry her through the Manhattan sky to a hovering spacecraft: the stories told by those who claim to have witnessed the event, rather than confirming her claim, make it more incredible.

Even if we accept that these events do indeed truly occur, we shall need to consider the possibility that they occur in some other sense than, say, our own astronauts' landing on the Moon. But if that is the case, what does it imply? Are there dimensions of space and time that parallel our own and intermittently interact with it, so that visitors shift from their reality into ours like someone stepping off an escalator onto solid ground? The moment we abandon the literal here-and-now consensus reality, which serves us so well in our everyday lives, we enter uncharted realms of metaphysical and spiritual possibility where anything that the human mind can conceive becomes possible.

Nevertheless, as we confront the stories told in this book, we must keep

such possibilities in mind. For whether or not we decide that the events really happened to Bernadette, Smith and Napolitano as they claim, there is no question but that *something* happened to them. There is more to these stories than fireside tales, wishful thinking, and private fantasy. Today's physics requires us to accept the paradoxical nature of reality, while notions of "virtual reality" show that although something is outside of common experience, it may still possess an objective validity of its own. On a different level to our everyday lives, it cannot be judged by the same rules.

Can spirits of the dead return to Earth from wherever it is we go to

when we die? Most would say that the question is meaningless because we aren't going anywhere, and the notion of survival is a biological absurdity. Even those who are willing to accept the notion of life after death dispute on theological grounds whether it is possible to return, even to make a brief ghostly appearance or materialize at a spirit seance. Are extraterrestrials able to cross the awesome distances of space to visit us? Scientists tell us it is so impractical as to be scarcely worth considering, except as an academic exercise. Nevertheless, when we are confronted with these and the other "impossible" stories that witnesses share with us, we must consider the possibility

*When, despite their prayers, San Gennaro fails to protect them from the 1872 eruption of Vesuvius, the populace attack his statue.*

*During World War One, the apparition of Thérèse of Lisieux guides French stretcher-bearers to where a soldier lies wounded.*

that they seem impossible to us only because they are taking place in some other dimension than the one we know.

# DIVINITIES AND DEMONS

For us today, to contemplate the reality or otherwise of otherworldly visits is an intellectual process: we assess the claims in the light of scientific principles. But, for our ancestors, it seems generally to have been a matter of simple, unquestioning belief. Even so, we are entitled to ask, how *literally* did our ancestors believe in these divine beings? Thunder and lightning are real enough – but were the deities which personified them anything more than convenient

abstractions? There seems little doubt that the man and woman in the street believed then, as many believe to this day, in the material existence of these beings and, moreover, that they actively participated in human affairs, manifesting in their physical presence if the case required it. When the volcano Etna threatens to erupt, Sicilian peasants pray to Sant' Egidius to save their villages from destruction, while those who live near Vesuvius trust in their local saint, San Gennario. In 1872 though, when he failed to answer their prayers and an eruption killed three people, they reproached him and attacked his statue. Evidently, for these unquestioning believers, the power they are invoking is not some theological abstraction, but a powerful individual who they are convinced has the power to save them. Their attitude to him is much like that of peasants in feudal times towards the local lord of the manor.

The ancient cultures best-known to us – Egypt, China, Mexico and Peru, classical Greece and Rome – possessed elaborate hierarchies of deities of greater or lesser importance. Each has his or her own attributes, kindly or menacing, helpful or vengeful. Each has a role to play on the cosmic stage. Some are vast in scope, creating worlds, ordering the galaxies. Others are more earthy. The Celtic goddess Brigid helps women to bear the pains of childbirth; the Chinese goddess Tse-Kou-Chen, a pious lady who was ignominiously murdered while on the toilet by a jealous rival, is consecrated Goddess of

the Privy and much honoured by her devotees for undertaking this humble but important position.

This tradition was carried over into more sophisticated religions. In the Roman Catholic version of Christianity it is believed that particular religious figures may be called upon to deal with particular problems. Saint Antony of Padua will help you find lost objects, while if your cause seems hopeless, you should call on Saint Jude. Many trades and professions honour patron saints who, it is supposed, will manifest on Earth and give them their protection – thus French bakers invoke Saint Honoré, and English shoemakers honour Saint Crispin.

During World War One, many such beings – saints, angels, Jesus and his mother Mary – made their appearance to encourage and comfort the warring warriors. Nor was their support confined to mere appearance. Some, like the gods in Homer's *Iliad*, played an active part. Thérèse of Lisieux, ten years before she was canonized, appeared on the Western Front and guided stretcher-bearers to where a French soldier was lying wounded.

For the Greeks and Romans, their pantheon of divinities was not very different from an Earthly royal court. The gods described by Homer indulge in power struggles and love affairs, jealousies, rivalries and warring ambitions, like any other ruling class. The gods and goddesses may possess superhuman powers, but their emotions and motivations are no more highly developed than ours. The Egyptian gods

*Tse-Kou-Chen, a concubine, murdered in the privy by her master's jealous legitimate wife, is rewarded by being appointed Goddess of the Privy.*

are pictured with the heads of dogs, birds or hippopotami, but for all that, they are as human in their behaviour as any dweller on Earth.

As religions grow more sophisticated, their divinities become less human, more remote. The gods become metaphysical abstractions, who are not perceived in human terms at all. Yet the tendency to anthropomorphize them persists. Throughout religious teachings, we persistently come across such phrases as "It is God's will that …", though in fact no one has the least idea of god's wishes or sentiments. The Christian belief-system cleverly manages to have it both ways. After his summit meeting with Moses, God remains in Heaven, but He sends an aspect of Himself, His "Son", to be born as a human being.

But where do these visitors, Jesus, Sainte Thérèse and the rest, actually come *from*? Where do the Gods dwell? Is there a Heaven, located somewhere in the Universe?

# HOMES OF THE GODS

The Gods of Homer's world don't live very far away. They can watch the progress of the Trojan War, and if they feel disposed to intervene, they simply pop down from the clouds. Just as the gods are not far removed from the human in appearance, so the places where they live are not very remote from our Earth.

Though from the start it was recognized that the gods could transcend the limitations of our earthly life, it was impossible to conceive of them existing outside space and time: they must live *somewhere*.

Early myths provided them with homes of their own here on Earth – in paradisal gardens, mountaintop citadels, island sanctuaries, underground caverns. If you sail sufficiently far into the Atlantic Ocean you may reach the Island of the Blest. If you climb Japan's Mount Fujiyama you may find yourself at the gateway to the next world. We have seen Moses ascend a mountain to receive the Ten Commandments. Sinai was the highest peak in the area, and by climbing it Moses was meeting God halfway, as it were. The body of King Arthur is carried in a boat to the enchanted isle of Avalon, whose inhabitants know all the magic of the world. When the Frankish King

*Heaven was not a distant place for the early Christians : a medieval missionary finds a place where Heaven touches Earth.*

Dagobert dies in the year 634, he is seized by demons who plan to take him to Hell, the entrance to which is via a volcano, specifically Mount Etna on the island of Sicily. Fortunately a posse of saints in shining white vestments repulse the demons as they sail across the Mediterranean, saving Dagobert for a less uncomfortable afterlife.

More generally, though, the homes of the gods are out of this world. Traditions worldwide presume the existence of a Heaven of some kind, and the more naive religions suppose that it has an actual location in space. If we set off into the cosmos in the right direction, we could get there. What we would find there, though, would not be so very different from what we are used to on Earth. Early Christian depictions of Heaven often showed it as a garden. In later, less pastoral times, it was compared to a celestial city, the New Jerusalem. Subsequently, the image of Heaven has not changed greatly. The "Summerland" – where, the spirits of the dead assured nineteenth-century

*When King Arthur is fatally wounded in battle, he is taken to the Island of Avalon, where he dies.*

spiritualist seance-goers, they were currently enjoying a blissful afterlife – is depicted as a lakeside park. The glimpses of gardens and cities of light given to those who undergo Near-Death Experiences are usually of indescribable beauty. The distant planets to which contactees are taken by the occupants of friendly spaceships are peaceful and well-ordered. All of them, rather than rivalling the fantasies of the science fiction artists, tend to resemble the nicer bits of the planet we know and love.

Wherever they are located, one attribute of the otherworlds remains constant – the *good* places, Heaven and its equivalents, are always perceived as *up there*, while the *bad* places, Hell and the like, are *down below*. When Jesus dies, he ascends to Heaven where a seat is reserved for him at the right hand of his father; when the rebel angels are routed by Saint Michael and the faithful angels, they are sent plunging down to an underworld which seems to have been prepared with their reception in mind. Christians believe that when they die they will go "up" to Heaven if they have been good, "down" to Hell if they have been bad. If they are Roman Catholics, they have a third alternative, Purgatory, where they can be cleansed of their wickedness and qualify for

Heaven.

Whether rewarded with Heaven or punished with Hell, the presumption is that the dead individual survives in some form. How much of us survives and how much we continue to be ourselves remain much-discussed questions, but allied with the notion that there are places designated Heaven and Hell is the notion that travel to and from them is possible. As we shall see later, return visits from the surviving dead, though under restricted conditions, form a significant category of otherworldly visits. Are the places where the gods reside, and the places where the spirits of the dead survive, one and the same? The experiences of some UFO contactees seem to confirm that this is the case. For example, on October 7, 1975, French motor-racing journalist Jean-Claude Vorilhon (aka "Raël") was taken by friendly extraterrestrials to their planet, described as "relatively close to Earth". There his host, Iahve, President of the Council, told him that there were 8400 Earthpeople now living on the planet, and, among the guests present at a party where they are entertained by naked female robot dancers, pointed out Moses, Jesus and other celebrities.

As culture progresses and religions develop, the homes of the gods come

*Airborne saints rescue Frankish king Dagobert from demons trying to carry him to Hell.*

to be seen as more remote. God, who had visited Earth when Adam and Eve were its only inhabitants and personally delivered the Ten Commandments to Moses, becomes a voice from the heavens, an abstract entity whose existence is a matter of faith rather than observation. However ,although we no longer expect God himself to come visiting, many Christians have no difficulty believing that Jesus, who once walked among us in the flesh, pays periodic return visits to specially privileged individuals. We shall come across instances of this in many different contexts. The case of Julie makes a good example.

Julie is a Star Person – that is, an Earthperson who has come to realize that she is in fact an extraterrestrial. She had always realized that she was "destined for some kind of special task", but just what this meant she had no idea until one night, while her husband was away on business, when she had the first of a sequence of visits from otherworldly beings. The first was an entity named Ashtar, an extraterrestrial ship commander well known to New Age channelers and UFO contactees. This entity remained in her home for *two years*, standing always in the same place. Nobody else was privileged to see him. Two days later, she had a second visitor – this time, it was Jesus, no less. She says he started projecting light beams on her, giving her an incredible feeling of total love. She describes her encounter in much the same terms as religious visionaries describe theirs. She lost consciousness, and when she woke Jesus had gone, leaving a golden light which has remained with her ever since.

Jesus, though, is a rather unique visitor; the frequency of his visits world-wide no doubt reflects the fact that he came from Heaven, took on human form and lived on Earth as a human. In most of the world's major religions though, either no travel takes place between here and there, or it is a one-way journey. The leading figure – Buddha, Mahomet, Zoroaster – gets to be transformed from a mortal into an immortal. The place of residence is no longer a paradisal garden or a celestial city, but some other plane of reality, whose nature is beyond our conception.

*Artists like the fifteenth-century Dirck Bouts depict Hell as a very real place – and a very uncomfortable one!*

**LEFT:** *The Hindu deity Vishnu takes a variety of forms ("avatars") for his periodic visits to Earth. Eighteenth-century image from Jaipur, Rajasthan.*

# VISITS FROM THE GODS

Any visits paid to Earth are occasional and brief. For the most part, heavenly beings stay in their heavens.

Even if such concepts are not taken literally by the more sophisticated belief-systems, the human mind does not find it easy to conceive of any form of existence that is not subject to space or time. How can it be "existence" if it doesn't happen somewhere, somewhen? So throughout human history, and for most people even today, divine beings are not abstractions on some other level of reality. Even if we no longer picture God – except in caricature, as a white-bearded old grandfather enthroned among the clouds – divinities still tend to be perceived as sufficiently like us that we could, given the appropriate circumstances, speak with them, interact with them, see them – even if it is only their back parts.

If gods exist, it is only natural that they would wish to inspect their property, much as a landowner goes round his estates; more so if they were also the creators of the Earth, yet more still if it was their one and only creation. The Christian Bible shows us a god very much concerned with His Earth and its inhabitants. There is no suggestion that He has created other races on other planets with whom He is equally concerned, and Jesus makes no mention of other species existing elsewhere in the universe.

So long as this was thought to be the case, visits from the gods were only to be expected, and early legends contain many accounts of such visits. Thus Vishnu, the supreme deity of the Hindus, is believed to have appeared on Earth in nine avatars, or incarnations, to help out when mankind has been threatened with some catastrophe engineered by malevolent forces.

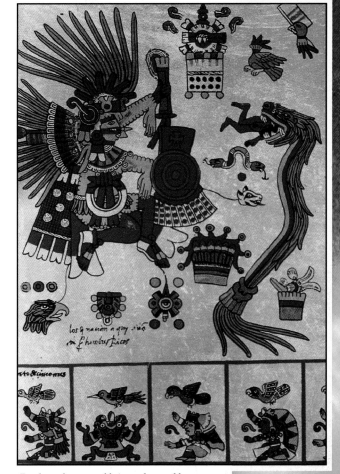

*For the gods were real beings who would come to Earth to reward the good and punish the wicked.*

The Aztecs of Mexico had a similar belief, but with rather more fatal consequences. They held a tradition that Quetzalcoatl, the god who had brought them knowledge of the arts and civilization, had landed at Vera Cruz and departed from there on a magic raft when his time with them was over. His return was much hoped for, and when Hernando Cortes and his conquistadors landed there in 1519 – coming from the same direction in their magnificent ships – the populace were eager to hail him as their hero-god. Cortes did not disabuse them, and their hesitation to see him as a dangerous enemy made his initial successes possible.

Hernando de Soto, in Peru, was able to benefit from a comparable tradition. The creator-god of the native Peruvians, Viracocha, had walked among them incognito, disguised as a beggar, performing miracles and instructing the people. He left Peru when the Spanish conquistadors crossed the Atlantic, walking away to the west on the waves of the Pacific, promising to return. A

*Despite his alarming appearance, Quetzalcoatl was a benevolent deity who brought learning and culture to the Aztec people.*

*Astronomer-priests of Ancient Egypt (c. 2880 BC) take advantage of the unique facilities of the Great Pyramid of Khufu as an observatory.*

prophecy stated that during the reign of the thirteenth Inca, "white men of surpassing strength and valour would come from their father the Sun, and subject the Peruvians to their rule". De Soto was content to be supposed to be their leader.

For most of us today, the gods no longer exist in their ancient form, if they exist at all. We do not expect them to visit us or revisit us. None the less, all those centuries of belief in otherworldly deities, of extramundane heavens and hells, have left their residue behind.

However sceptical we may be, at the back of all our minds is the vague notion that other worlds may exist, populated by other beings. Visionary encounters with divine beings are reported as frequently as ever, and while most of us no longer look for the gods or the saints to intervene in human affairs, the "Second Coming" of Jesus is an article of faith for some fundamentalist Christians. Stories of angels found a renewed popularity as the twentieth century ended, and, like devils and demons, we shall see that they have been amongst the most persistent of all our visitors.

# THE ONLY CREATION?

Faith is all very well, but it's always reassuring to have it propped up by fact. So long as it was believed that the homes of the gods and the demons were physical places, locating Heaven and Hell was a practical problem which the scientists of the day could reasonably be called upon to solve. That the stars and planets play a significant part in human affairs was a central tenet in many early religions.

The Priests of Chaldea and Egypt became astronomers also, and science served as the handmaid of religion, observing the Heavens. Hell interested them less, being buried beneath the ground, approachable via volcanoes, and in any case offering few attractions as a tourist destination. But the gods, if they lived anywhere, lived among the stars.

By far the most prominent of the celestial bodies – indeed, the only ones which can be seen by the naked eye to possess any bulk whatever – are the Sun and Moon. It is not surprising that Sun Gods and Lunar Deities are among the most honoured of divinities, and that both have been the subject of widespread worship in every part of the world. The Sun god Re was one of the most powerful of Egyptian deities; for the Bacongo people of Zaire, the solar deity Nzambi is judge, protector, sustainer of the universe; and, for the Greeks, Apollo personified this dynamic life force.

As theology grew more sophisticated, "Heaven" came to be perceived as not so much a place as a state of grace in which we mortals, freed from our physical bodies and transfigured into some superior form, are absorbed into a divine super-being. When God became a spiritual abstraction, no longer likely to visit Earth in person, there was no longer any need to imagine him actually living anywhere. The idea of Heaven and Hell as places capable of being physically located on a map of the universe no longer seemed appropriate. But the visible celestial bodies, the Sun and more probably the Moon, remained possibly inhabited by other kinds of being. Old mythologies had included a variety of beings who were neither gods nor humans – Titans, giants, sphinxes, djinns and other monsters of land, sea and air. In the minds of those who made imaginary journeys to the Moon, the traveller must be prepared to meet creatures very unlike humanity. Mankind was learning to stretch its imagination.

The earliest accounts of imaginary journeys into space were not intended to be taken literally – if they were supposed to be considered seriously, it was as moral documents rather than travel accounts. Writing in the second century AD, Loukianos of Samosata told, in his *True history* – a satire on travellers' tales – how his ship was caught up by a whirlwind which swept their vessel up "some three thousand furlongs" (about 600 km) into the air, where all were able to observe the Moon and its inhabitants. The description is pure fancy. There are no women, for the young are born from the thighs of their fathers. They drink air, and take out their eyes as though they are eyeglasses. In short, this is fantasy rather than scientific conjecture.

A quite different account is given by Loukianos's near-contemporary, Plutarch, whose imaginary description is a mixture of intelligent speculation and utter credulity. What is interesting is that he is convinced the Moon *is* inhabited. As evidence, he cites the fall of the Lion of Nemea, which plunged from the Moon into the Greek Peloponnese. Other accounts enliven the theological writings of the day. The Christian theologian Origen wonders what Saint Matthew meant when he wrote

> ... his angels shall gather his elect from the four winds, from one end of heaven to the other ...

and concludes that this points to a literal Heaven where the dead reside, having physical dimensions. The Jewish religious book, the *Zohar*, refers to "the God of all worlds known and unknown" – some take this as evidence for the plurality of inhabited worlds. A sixth-century legend tells of three monks who travel in search of Paradise, stray beyond the edge of the world and eventually find it. The Italian poet Dante, on Good Friday 1300, is led by the spirit of the Roman writer Virgil into the Inferno where the damned are tortured everlastingly, and is given a glimpse of Paradise by his beloved Beatrice. Ariosto and Rabelais are just two of the eminent writers who interpolate space voyages into their writings.

But none of these, however fine as literature, can be considered as in any way a serious document, and their authors are careful to present their ideas as fantasies, moral fables or satires on Earthly lifestyles. The penalties for not doing so tended to be serious. The Italian philosopher Giordano Bruno was burnt to death in 1600 for spreading the loathsome heresy that our Earth is not the centre of the cosmos, but just one small world in an infinitely large universe.

Hundreds of these scattered hints tell us that people everywhere were casting thoughtful eyes to the heavens,

*The Lion of Nemea, according to ancient Greek legends, fell to the Peloponnese from the Moon. From Flammarion's* Histoire du Ciel *(Story of the Sky).*

and often the consequence was that another fantastic tale was added to the literature. But none added to our stock of scientific knowledge, and none hinted that, just as we thought about visiting other worlds, so people of other worlds might be thinking of visiting Earth.

# MORE WORLDS THAN ONE

In the year 1609, mankind's view of the universe changed dramatically. The Italian astronomer, Galileo, recognizing the potential of the recently invented telescope, adapted it for observation of the heavens – the first effective use of the device for astronomical purposes. Though only a handful of scholars were even aware of the discovery, let alone able to grasp its implications, this was nevertheless a turning point in man's conception of the cosmos. Nothing would ever be the same again. For what Galileo sees through his crude instrument confirms that the theological view of creation, in which our Earth is the centre of the universe and mankind is God's special creation, is no longer tenable. The sky can now be seen to be filled with other worlds – worlds which may be like our own, even inhabited by people like ourselves.

*The Italian poet Dante Alighieri enjoys an otherworld journey when his beloved Beatrice gives him a vision of Paradise.*

The discovery sparked off a new era of excited speculation. Scientists and philosophers alike felt authorized to consider the possibility of other inhabited worlds, and book after book came off the press debating the matter. Some authors, such as Pierre Borel, physician to the French court – whose 1647 book was entitled *A New discourse proving the plurality of worlds, that the stars are inhabited worlds, and that the Earth is a star, etc.* – gave the question serious consideration. Borel based his reasoning on the new discoveries:

> But Galileo who, within our own lifetime, has seen clearly into the Moon, has observed that it could well be inhabited, seeing that there are mountains and plains there.

Others were more fanciful. Among Borel's contemporaries was the satirist Cyrano de Bergerac, who, in his 1649 book *Histoire Comique des Etat et Empire de la Lune*, told how he placed flasks of dew round his waist at night. When the sun rose, it caused the dew to rise, enabling him to be lifted through the skies to the Moon.

The English writer Francis Godwin published his *Man in the Moone* in 1638, which purported to be written by one Domingo Gonsales, but this is no more than a literary device. It tells how he trained wild swans to tow a burden through the air. Then, like the Montgolfier brothers in the following century, and the Russian space programme two centuries after that, he experimented first with animals. He got his trained swans to make an aerial voyage drawing a lamb "whose happiness I much envied, that he should be the first living creature to take possession of such a device". Needless to say, one thing led to another, and soon he himself had occasion to make serious use of his device, when his ship was wrecked and he escaped thanks to his birds.

An even stranger adventure awaited him. Earlier he had wondered why this species of birds disappeared for a period of the year; now he learned that it was because of their hibernation. They spent part of every year in the Moon. When the time to hibernate came, they set off for the Moon,

*Science and poetry meet: the Italian astronomer Galileo, under house arrest in Florence,*
*is visited by the English poet John Milton, in 1638/9.*

carrying Gonsales with them. As the air grew thinner, they escaped the Earth's pull, so the birds had no trouble carrying him such a distance. On the Moon he discovered giant Lunarians, whose society and lifestyle was vastly superior to those on Earth.

Such fantasies may not add much to scientific knowledge, but they fanned popular interest. When in 1686 Bernard Le Bovier de Fontenelle published his *Conversations on the plurality of worlds*, he imagined himself walking in a park after supper with an intelligent noblewoman for company. The marquise questioned him about what they could see in the sky above their heads, and he was delighted to have a willing audience for his explanations. He did not think that other worlds contained people like ourselves, but that each would be peopled by beings suitable to the prevailing conditions. Though, as he was the first to say, all he can do is speculate, this was not satire or science fiction, but true speculation as to life on other worlds – what kind of life, and how it would cope with the problems of existence elsewhere. For example:

What do we know but that the inhabitants of the Moon, incommoded by the perpetual heat of the Sun, do not hide in deep wells, perhaps building their cities there. The entire race lives there, moving from one well to another by subterranean passages.

As technology improves, so Man's knowledge of the universe increases and the possibility of other life-forms becomes a stronger possibility. But at that time, the question was merely an academic one – a game of the imagination, with no practical application. In his 1647 book, Borel had written:

Some have thought that just as man has imitated the fish by swimming, so he can equally learn to fly, and by this means resolve the question [whether there are other inhabited worlds]. History reports many examples of men who have flown. But even if man should learn to fly, it will do him little service, for, apart from the fact that, due to his weight, man will not be able to rise high, nor will he be able to stop to study the other worlds, but all his spirit will be directed on controlling his machine.

But the rapid advance of technology was to prove Borel unnecessarily pessimistic – we have risen high indeed, and have studied other worlds.

*Galileo's telescope and other instruments,*
*preserved in the Museo delle Scienze, Florence.*

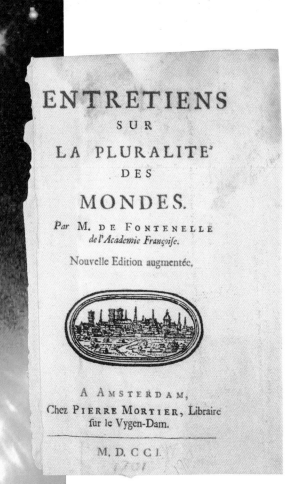

*In Fontenelle's 1686 book* Entretiens sur la Pluralié des Mondes, *he discusses with a marquise the probability of extraterrestrial life.*

# MAN LEAVES HIS PLANET

The first aerial voyage – a brief flight over Paris by Pilâtre de Rozier and the Maréchal d'Arlandes in a Montgolfier hot-air balloon on November 21, 1783 – marked a further dramatic change to thinking. Though the journey was a very brief one, and Earth was never more than a few hundred metres below, the achievement was of overwhelming significance. For the first time, man was able to look down on his planet and see it as a visitor from other worlds might see it.

Now, for the first time, travel beyond Earth could be conceived not just as a fantasy, but as a serious possibility. Throughout the century that followed, thousands of inventors throughout the world developed the concept of flight in many directions – many of them foolish and fruitless, but some containing the seeds of future developments. Running ahead of them were the authors of science fiction, which became less fantasy and satire, and more a projection of what are now seen as scientific realities.

Jules Verne's 1865 publication *Autour de la Lune (Round the Moon)* and its 1870 sequel *De la Terre à la Lune (From the Earth to the Moon)* were landmark works. For the first time, serious consideration was given to the "space ship", though Verne's picture of a projectile with its padded walls and Victorian furnishings is somewhat less than scientific. The fact that he installs padded walls at all shows that he had given serious thought to the problems that accompany weightlessness. On the other hand his proposed solution for enabling the projectile to escape the attraction of Earth's gravity – a huge cannon buried in the ground, from which the space ship is fired like a military shell – was naive, to put it kindly. Congreve's rockets, demonstrated in 1827, offered a far more realistic solution.

Verne's books were aimed at a popular audience, and what was significant was the way the idea of space travel had now become an idea that everyone could toy with, not simply an academic game for sophisticated writers. Though the notion of space travel was evidently an idea whose time had come, much of the credit for turning it from academic game-playing to a popular notion must be given to Camille Flammarion, a French astronomer of repute. In his *Les Mondes Imaginaires* of 1866 he surveyed the history of man's developing notions of extraterrestrial worlds, and throughout the remaining decades of the nineteenth century he followed it with a series of books and articles in which he proposed, discussed and championed the idea that ours is not the only inhabited world in the universe. Translated into many languages, his well-informed opinions carried great weight, and were an inspiration to many writers who pioneered the genre which would later be labelled 'science fiction'.

# LETTERS FROM THE PLANETS

*Cassell's Family Magazine* was a sober and respectable publication intended to entertain and instruct the middle class households of England. Its pages were filled with domestic advice, nature studies and moral stories about good girls who triumphed over difficulties to win the man of their heart. How astonished its readers must have been when they opened the issue for February 1887, to find the first of a series of papers entitled "Letters from the Planets". If we today are bewildered to find accounts of extraterrestrial abduction appearing beside the recipes and marital counsel in our weekly magazines, imagine how much more amazing it must have seemed to a family in Victorian England.

The letters purported to be written not by the author, an English country gentleman, but by an extraterrestrial friend of his named Aleriel, who supposed – reasonably enough – that an account of his travels would interest an Earthperson. He told of visiting the

**RIGHT:** *On November 21, 1783, Pilâtre de Rozier and the Marquis d'Arlandes make the first successful manned flight, in a hot air balloon.*

DE LA TIERRA A LA LUNA

JULIO VERNE

E. Freixas

*Jules Verne's 1865 story* From the Earth to the Moon *catches the imagination of the world; this Spanish edition is one of many translations.*

Moon, where he indeed found traces of former life, but now only ruins remain. On the other hand, when he visited Mars, he found it teeming with life and bustling with activity. The Martian cities were built on islands which floated on the surface of the canals. Aleriel was excited by:

... this huge masterpiece of the marvellous skill and power of the Martians – an achievement as far superior to any man has yet achieved in this age of steam and iron, as the works of human skill in the nineteenth century are superior to the works of man in the Stone Age.

In supposing that life on Mars was more advanced than here on Earth, the author was voicing the general opinion. H G Wells pointed out that Mars is considerably older than Earth, and being smaller would have cooled more rapidly, so that conditions capable of supporting life would have appeared while our own planet was still a mass of molten rock. With such a start, it was only to be expected that the Martian civilization would be superior to ours.

Besides, there are the famous canals as evidence. In his brilliant fantasy *To Mars via the Moon*, Mark Wicks depicted the canals as clearly Martian-

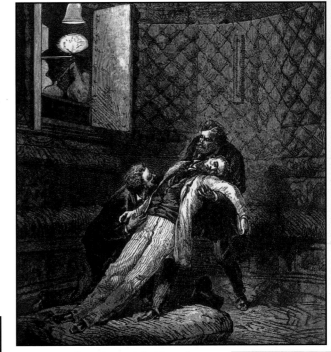

*In Verne's 1870 sequel,* Round the Moon, *the travellers recover from the shock of blast-off.*

made, linking town to town as do our autoroutes. True, not everyone agreed with the American astronomer Percival Lowell that they were artificial constructions, but whatever they were, they were the most prominent physical feature on the planet, and encouraged the hope that life may exist there.

"The hope"? While the idea that there might be life elsewhere in the universe is an exciting one, it is by no means sure that those who share the cosmos with us will be friendly. It might be prudent to be on one's guard ...

One day in the 1890s, HG Wells was walking with his brother Frank, when their conversation turned to the people of Tasmania, and how astonished they must have been by the arrival of the first Europeans. "Imagine," observed Frank, "how we would react if beings from another planet were to drop from the sky and install themselves here".

That remark provided the starting-point for what is possibly the finest science fiction story ever written – *The War of the Worlds*. The story opens with these splendidly ominous words which, in themselves, show how much more sophisticated man's ideas about his place in the cosmos had become:

No one would have believed, in the last years of the nineteenth century, that

*This imaginary scene on a distant planet, illustrating Flammarion's best-selling* Astronomie populaire, *encouraged the public of 1881 to take seriously the idea of travel to other worlds.*

human affairs were being watched keenly and closely by intelligences greater than man's and yet as mortal as his own; that as men busied themselves about their affairs they were scrutinized and studied, perhaps almost as narrowly as a man with a microscope might scrutinize the transient creatures that swarm and multiply in a drop of water … No one gave a thought to the older worlds of space as sources of human danger … At most, terrestrial men fancied there might be other men upon Mars, perhaps inferior to themselves and ready to welcome a missionary enterprise. Yet, across the gulf of space, minds that are to our minds as ours are to those of the beasts, intellects vast and cool and unsympathetic,

regarded this earth with envious eyes, and slowly and surely drew their plans against us …

As Wells tells his story, mankind quickly learns that the Martians are distinctly unfriendly. But they were also – and this was a turning-point in the development of the Martian myth – distinctly *non-human*. Previous writers had conceived of extraterrestrials as being more or less variations on humankind. After all, the Bible tells us that man was created in the image of God, and it must be supposed that other races would enjoy the same privilege. Yet, though the various artists who have illustrated Wells' book and the film-

*RIGHT: David Hardy's painting reflects the technological superiority of Wells' Martians.*

makers who have created screen versions differ widely in their interpretation of what the Martians are like, all are agreed on one thing – Wells's Martians are not a bit like us.

But is Wells right? During the early years, at least, authors and artists were not so sure that the Martians would be monsters. Later we shall be looking more closely at changing fashions in extraterrestrial style. For the moment though, let us simply note that while Wells undoubtedly set a fashion with *The War of the Worlds*, not every author

*Readers of* Cassell's Family Magazine *in March 1889 must have been astonished by this illustration showing a Venusian spacecraft flying over Mars at night.*

# AMAZING STORIES

## SEPTEMBER

**25 Cents**

felt bound to assume that visiting aliens would be unfriendly. Then as now, some feared the worst from encounters with other worlds, and some hoped for the best.

# AMAZING STORIES

Hugo Gernsback (1884–1967) was born in Luxembourg, and emigrated to the USA at the age of twenty. As early as 1916 he was writing articles with such titles as "Thought transmission on Mars". In 1926 he launched the magazine *Amazing Stories*, the first of a number of periodicals which have been variously termed "comics" and "pulps" but deserve a more respectful label. Later came *Air Wonder Stories, Science Wonder Stories* and others, all featuring what he called "scientifiction". The slogan printed on every title page of *Amazing Stories* – "Extravagant Fiction Today – Cold Fact Tomorrow" neatly expressed his belief that what his authors drew from their imaginations, later generations would put into practice. In a 1927 editorial, he wrote:

> The editors of AMAZING STORIES are trying their best to keep from this magazine stories that belong rather in the domain of fairy tales than of scientifiction. The editorial board makes this fine distinction: a story, to be true scientifiction, should have a scientific basis of plausibility, so that while it may not seem possible to perform the miracle this year or next, it may conceivably come about 500, 5000 or 500,000 years hence.

Because they paid poorly, the pulps did not attract the best writers in the genre, but the sheer bulk of their output ensured that a great many variations on the basic themes were produced, often with remarkable ingenuity. What distinguishes these stories is not the quality of their prose but the inventiveness of their ideas. Between them, these hundreds of authors, most

*Illustrating one of Gernsback's own stories, this spacecraft of 1929 anticipates later "flying saucers."*

of whose names are now forgotten except by connoisseurs of the genre, anticipated almost every idea that was later to manifest in the flying saucer myth. This included not only alien spacecraft of every conceivable shape and size, but also their occupants, no less diverse, along with abduction by aliens, immobilisation by ray-guns, physical examination of victims strapped on operating tables, cloning and brainwashing.

In particular, the theme which concerns us here – visits to Earth by extraterrestrials – was covered from almost every conceivable angle. One frequent theme was that our planet had something which other worlds lack. In Eando Binder's *The thieves from Isot* [1934] invaders from Pluto come to mine the Earth for malachite, a substance they need for their technology. More frequently, though, it's our entire planet they are after. The title of Isaac Nathanson's *The Conquest of the Earth* [1930] announces its theme. Huge reptilian creatures from Andromeda

seize control of the planet but are of course ultimately repulsed. In Don Stuart's *The Invaders* [1935], the Tharoos, a race of big-headed humanoids of superior intelligence, colonize Earth, treating humanity as farm animals.

In John W Campbell's *When the atoms failed* (1930), a massive landing of Martians seems certain of success until an Earth scientist develops a ray which blasts their spaceships out of the sky. In P Schuyler Miller's *Tetrahedra of Space* (1931), crystalline beings from Mercury land in South America. Fortunately they are allergic to water, and when Earth people explain how much of Earth's surface is covered with the deadly liquid, they depart to try their luck elsewhere.

Sometimes their visit is motivated by simple curiosity – the 50-kilometre long spacecraft which lands in the Russian Steppes in 1995 in Stanton A Coblentz's *The Golden Planetoid* (1935) shows no indication of aggression, and stays on Earth as long as it does only because it is damaged when landing and needs to be

*Alien invaders: in John W Campbell's 1930 story, the Martians are once again Earth's natural enemy.*

## "WHAT TIME WILL IT BE THE END OF THE WORLD?"

It is significant that the golden age of science fiction should culminate in an incident in which fantasy impinged on real life so forcefully that it was actually perceived as reality. The Columbia Broadcasting System's radio production of H G Wells' *War of the Worlds* on the evening of October 30, 1938 was a remarkable demonstration of what can happen when the dividing edge between fact and fiction becomes blurred.

The radio show was only one hour long, and contained incidents which would have required, at the very least, several hours to occur in fact. However, so besotted were the listeners with the *idea* of what they were hearing, they abandoned even the most fundamental notions of reality testing. The following morning, under the headline "RADIO LISTENERS IN PANIC, TAKING WAR DRAMA AS FACT", the *New York Times* reported:

> The radio listeners, apparently, missed or did not listen to the introduction, which was "The Columbia Broadcasting System and its affiliated stations present Orson Welles and the Mercury Theatre on the Air in 'The War of the Worlds' by H G Wells".
>
> They also failed to associate the program with the newspaper listing of the program. They ignored three additional announcements made during the broadcast emphasizing its fictional nature.

At least 6 million listeners heard the broadcast, and subsequent research established that over a million of them had been frightened or disturbed. For many, it was more than that. Thousands of those listening became firmly convinced that Martians had actually landed in New Jersey, and that they represented a dire and immediate threat to humanity. The *New York Times* gave many specific instances of the panic:

repaired. But even a non-aggressive mission can be misinterpreted. Eando Binder's *The Robot Aliens* (1935) tells the sad story of robots sent from Mars who are instantly perceived as enemies by Earth authorities, though they use no weapons and cause no damage. Several people are killed as the result of their visit, but only through panic or in the course of aggression by Earth's security forces. One robot survives long enough to explain matters to an Earthman who befriends and hides it, but in the end he and the robot are both killed by villagers who suspect another Frankenstein creating a monster like they've seen at the movies.

Binder's moral intention in that story is evident, and several science fiction stories try to counter the image created by Wells, where aliens are self-evidently hostile. In W K Sonnerman's *Master Minds of Venus* (1934), the visiting Venerians [sic] come to Earth specifically for the purpose of helping us. Their intentions are misunderstood, and the conflict is between Earthpeople who want to destroy the aliens and those who recognize their goodwill.

W P Cockcroft, in *The Alien Room* (1934), goes one step further. When climbers on Mount Everest find an abandoned alien spacecraft containing the skeleton of its occupant, they enter it, toy with the controls, and are sent hurtling back to the alien world leaving only their companion – who hadn't entered with them – to tell their story.

• A wave of mass hysteria seized thousands of radio listeners throughout the nation between 8.15 and 9.30 o'clock last night when a broadcast of a dramatization of H G Wells's fantasy, "The War of the Worlds", led thousands to believe that an interplanetary conflict had started with invading Martians spreading wide death and destruction in New Jersey and New York …

• In Newark, in a single block, more than twenty families rushed out of their houses with wet handkerchiefs and towels over their heads to protect them from what they believed was to be a gas raid. Throughout New York families left their homes, some to flee to near-by parks. Thousands of persons called the police, newspapers and radio stations, seeking advice on protective measures against the raids.

• Large numbers asked how they could follow the broadcast's advice and flee from the city, whether they would be safer from the "gas raid" in the cellar or on the roof, how they could safeguard their children.

• One man who called from Dayton, Ohio, asked "What time will it be the end of the world?" and a lady who called the bus company explained to the operator that "the world is coming to an end and I have a lot to do".

A notable feature of the event was the way in which rumours, totally divorced from even the radio play, sprang up. A man rushed into a New York police station shouting that "enemy planes" were crossing the Hudson River and asking what he should do. Many persons stood on street corners hoping for a sight of the "battle in the skies", while elsewhere one fugitive found "hundreds of people milling about in panic". A phone call to a police station asked "if the wave of poison gas will reach as far as Queens". In college dormitories, students waited in line to "take their turn at the telephone to make long distance calls to their parents, saying goodbye for what they thought might be the last time".

A Newark hospital treated fifteen men and women for shock and hysteria. At nearby Caldwell an excited parishioner ran into the First Baptist Church during evening service and shouted that a meteor had fallen, showering death and destruction. One caller went onto his roof to check the story that "they're bombing New Jersey" and claimed "I could see the smoke from the bombs, drifting over toward New York". Another said "I stuck my head out of the window and thought I could smell the gas. And it felt as though it was getting hot, like fire was coming". Yet another: "I looked out of my window and saw a greenish eerie light which I was sure came from a monster. Later on it proved to be the lights in the maid's car."

The interweaving of fiction and reality is explicit in this witness statement:

At first I was very interested in the fall of the meteor. But when it started to unscrew and monsters came out, I said to myself, "They've taken one of those Amazing Stories and are acting it out". It just couldn't be real. It was just like some of the stories I read in *Amazing Stories* but it was even more exciting.

## "Mass Hysteria"?

This remarkable episode inspired widespread comment from observers of social behaviour, professional and amateur. "Mass hysteria" provided a convenient label, but it was only a label, not an explanation. Journalist Dorothy Thompson, writing in the *New York Herald Tribune* on November 2, wrote that "nothing whatever about the dramatization was in the least credible" and blamed the panic on the "incredible

*The first Martian emerges – one of Alvin Correa's classic illustrations to H G Wells' War of the Worlds.*

*76-year old William Dock stands ready with loaded shotgun to repel the Martian invaders of New Jersey.*

Europe and a period in which the radio frequently has interrupted regularly scheduled programs to report developments in the Czechoslovak situation, caused fright and panic throughout the area of the broadcast.

The Nazi invasion of Czechoslovakia had precipitated an international crisis, and though temporarily defused, the threat of World War Two was hanging over the world. It must surely have been at the back of the mind of many of those listening, and some people articulated it.

One panicking listener reported, "I knew it was some Germans trying to gas all of us. When the announcer kept calling them people from Mars I just thought he was ignorant and didn't know yet that Hitler had sent them all". Another said:

> The announcer said a meteor had fallen from Mars, and I was sure he thought that, but in back of my head I had the idea that the meteor was just a camouflage. It was really an aeroplane like a Zeppelin that looked like a meteor and the Germans were attacking us with gas bombs. The aeroplane was built to look like a meteor just to fool people.

Summarizing his findings, Cantril concluded:

> Critical ability alone is not a sure preventive of panic. It may be overpowered either by an individual's own susceptible personality or by emotions generated in him by an unusual listening situation.

stupidity" of the panicking listeners.

Sociologists disagreed. Hadley Cantril, professor of psychology at Princeton and author of the definitive study of the episode, demonstrated that intelligence or stupidity were secondary factors at best. Instead, he identified three factors:

1. critical ability – the ability to test for reality.
2. personal susceptibility – some people are more suggestible than others.
3. the listening situation – the actual context in which the broadcast was heard.

No one of these three on its own was likely to cause a person to panic. For most people in most situations, possession of critical ability is sufficient insurance against being deceived. But people are not all alike. Some have a lower suggestibility threshold than others, and more easily accept what they think they see. We believe that testing for reality is an instinctive process, but circumstances may override it. Cantril found that 1 in 3 of those who panicked made no attempt to check, whether by phoning the authorities, switching to another radio channel, or checking with friends or neighbours.

Outside circumstances can play a critical part. An important factor in the Martian episode was the prevailing political climate. The *New York Times* accurately identified one important factor:

> Despite the fantastic nature of the reported "occurrences", the program, coming after the recent war scare in

We would do well to bear Cantril's finding in mind throughout this survey of otherworldly visitations, for what he says of the Martian panic is applicable to a wide range of experiences. What the incident demonstrated was that you don't have to be stupid, or mentally ill, or in any other way exceptional, to be placed by circumstances in a situation where you fail, or are unable, to make a distinction between fantasy and fact. If conditions favour it, a substantial portion of the population may hallucinate, misinterpret events or be deluded out of common reality.

While it would be illegitimate to suggest that this is always the case in any report of otherworldly visitation, it is a possibility that we should always keep in mind, whether we are concerned with contact from spirits of the dead or with abduction by extraterrestrials.

Clearly, though, any such possibility was far from Orson Welles' mind. Commenting the next day, he disclosed that, far from anticipating panic, he feared the radio audience might not be sufficiently entertained:

> It was our thought that perhaps people might be bored or annoyed at hearing a tale so improbable.

Like many before and since, Orson Welles underestimated humanity's ability to create a myth, and, having created it, to mistake it for reality.

## FROM MOSES TO MARTIANS

It seems a far cry from God speaking with Moses on Mount Sinai to Martians landing in New Jersey. But both episodes are the expression of belief, whether founded or not. If no facts, or insufficient facts are available, then we will fill the gap with fantasy, surmise and speculation. Our hopes and fears will direct our thoughts towards saviours or monsters. Myths and legends will be created, rumours will fly. An example of this process at work can be seen in the "cargo cults" that occur among the peoples of the South Pacific. From time to time on the scattered islands of the Pacific, a belief will arise that otherworldly beings are about to bestow on the native population the goods that have been held from them by the selfish white man. In his book, *John Frum, He Come*, Edward Rice writes.

> South Pacific Cargo received its greatest impetus during World War II, after the arrival of American troops landed on dozens of islands with unlimited types of western goods, from war materials to … candy bars … whiskey and other luxuries undreamed of by people scarcely out of the stone age.

Mankind looks to the otherwordly beings for many reasons. Some are as material as the South Sea Islanders hoping for candy bars and whiskey, others are looking for spiritual reassurance or for confirmation of their worst fears. But in one sense or another we are all looking for our share of the "Cargo".

*The day after the broadcast, producer Orson Welles defends his production against a storm of media and popular criticism.*

# Aerial Beings

**"We live at the bottom of an atmospheric ocean. Is it possible that other organisms may live above us? If the seas of our Earth are swarming with varieties of living things, both great and small, is it not logical to assume that the 'sea' of our sky abounds with sundry forms of living things, likewise both great and small, of varied shapes, but adaptable to their celestial environment?"**

So wrote American author John Philip Bessor in 1955. Similarly, in 1983 the astronomer Fred Hoyle wrote:

> To me it seemed preposterous that NASA should be spending hundreds of millions of dollars in a mission to discover if there was life on Mars, while leaving unresolved the question of whether there was life a mere 50 kilometres (30 miles) above our heads.

The idea that Earth's atmosphere may sustain its own race of beings, independent of life on the planet's surface, is one which has intrigued many speculative thinkers. Although there is little evidence to support the idea, there have been some tantalizing hints.

In 1917, during the First World War, a strange story was submitted by an anonymous airman to a very respectable monthly, *The Occult Review*. The writer told of an unusual experience by a fellow aviator, who did not wish his name to be cited in connection with so strange a story, but who is described as "a very experienced airman":

> He told me confidentially that at a very great height he had seen a curious coloured dragon-like animal apparently floating in the air and approaching him

rapidly. Understandably, the pilot had become a little unnerved and at once descended to earth; but for fear of being ridiculed and accused of over-indulgence in alcoholic refreshment he had said nothing. Had it been an isolated experience, he might have ended by doubting his own eyes: but that first sighting was confirmed by subsequent experiences of the same kind. He suspected that other pilots may have had similar experiences, but like him were reluctant to tell their stories for fear of being laughed at by their colleagues.

Well, a story told by one unnamed aviator to another does not carry much scientific weight. What makes this one particularly interesting is that it seems to have been anticipated a few years earlier by none other than the creator of Sherlock Holmes. Conan Doyle's fictional story "The Horror of the Heights" was published in the popular weekly *The Strand*, in its November 1913 issue. Though told with Doyle's usual vivid touches and convincing detail, it makes no pretensions to be anything other than an exciting piece of science fiction. It is a typical example of the speculative writing with which H G Wells and others were thrilling the reading public.

The story tells of an aviator who is determined to explore the upper atmosphere in his flimsy monoplane, a machine pretty much like the plane in which Louis Bleriot had crossed the Channel only four years earlier. Flying at about 12,000 metres (40,000 ft) the hero encounters

> the most wonderful vision that ever man has seen … Conceive a jellyfish such as sails in our summer seas – far larger than the dome of St Paul's cathedral. It was of a light pink colour veined with a delicate green: from it there descended two long drooping tentacles …

It becomes clear that these are living creatures that are inhabiting the upper

*LEFT: A mysterious ball of light shines brightly above the earth. Could our own atmosphere contain lifeforms unknown to us?*

*An aviator flying at 12,000 metres (40,000 ft) above the the earth encounters mysterious life forms in Conan Doyle's* Horror of Heights.

atmosphere. Beautiful they may be, but they are also dangerous. They resent the intruder from Earth's surface, who barely manages to escape their evidently hostile manoeuvres.

Despite their hostility, however, he is determined to continue his explorations. Leaving behind the record of his first encounter – which provides the basis for Doyle's story – he sets off again, but this time he is never seen again. He disappears, along with his plane, to a fate unknown. Doyle can only speculate that he "had been overtaken and devoured by these horrible creatures at some spot in the outer atmosphere".

Doyle was writing simply to entertain us, and it would be reasonable to suppose that his fantasy possesses even less substance than the story by the anonymous contributor to *The Occult Review*. However, not for the first time, it seems a science fiction writer was ahead of the scientists themselves.

In July 1993 two NASA observers flying above a thunderstorm made a major contribution to meteorology when they scientifically established a fact that had long been reported by flyers. Not all lightning flashes are from the clouds to the earth: they occur also above the clouds, rising rather than descending.

The NASA observers logged 19 flashes, but it was the term they used to describe them which concerns us. They likened them to – of all things – jellyfish:

> They appear brightest where they top out, typically about 65 kilometres (40 miles) high, so you have the jellyfish body at the top with tentacles trailing down.

Was this what the World War One aviator saw and what Doyle was describing in his fiction? But if so, how could he possibly know that the mysterious "aerial dragons" would resemble jellyfish? For at that time, no aircraft had been constructed capable of reaching an altitude where an aviator could have seen this phenomenon at first hand.

*"In the Abyss", by HG Wells, told of divers encountering strange creatures in the ocean, asking us to entertain the idea that intelligent life may exist parallel to our own civilization.*

GOLD KEY®

90259-211

UFO FLYING SAUCERS

15c

# UFO FLYING SAUCERS

ARE THEY ALIVE?
STRANGE EVENTS—OMINOUS ENCOUNTERS—
THAT CONFRONT AND BAFFLE MANKIND!

# A "SPACE-AGE" MYTH

There was a wave of sightings of mystery airships across the USA during the 1890s, a time when experimentation with flying machines was widespread. Another airship scare occurred in Britain just before the First World War, perhaps in response to general apprehension of the imminent hostilities. And the first craft to be dubbed a 'flying saucer' – in fact several such craft – were first sighted in Washington State in June 1947, just at the time when we inhabitants of Earth were making our first tentative ventures into the cosmos.

Is the entire flying saucer phenomenon a fantasy generated by our space age preoccupations? If the cluster of encounter tales described above were fantasies created by the cultural climate, then could not 'flying saucers' be the same?

This was the conclusion reached by one of the few people to have played a part in both the turn-of-the-century "Martian Scare" and the latter-day "Age of the Flying Saucer": the Swiss psychologist Carl Gustav Jung. His book *Flying Saucers: A Modern Myth of Things Seen in the Skies* remains one of the most perceptive commentaries on the UFO phenomenon. This is despite the fact that it was written when that phenomenon was only ten years old, when the case file was only a fraction of its present size. Some of the most striking features of the UFO phenomenon – including the remarkable outbreak of abduction claims – had yet to occur. Nevertheless, patterns were already beginning to emerge. Jung notes how often the report insists that

> the witness is above suspicion because he was never distinguished for his lively imagination or credulousness but, on the contrary, for his cool judgement and critical reason.

LEFT: *Brigadier General Roger M Ramey, commanding officer of the 8th Airforce, and Colonel Thomas Dubose, 8th Airforce Chief of Staff, look over the balloon debris found at Roswell in 1947.*

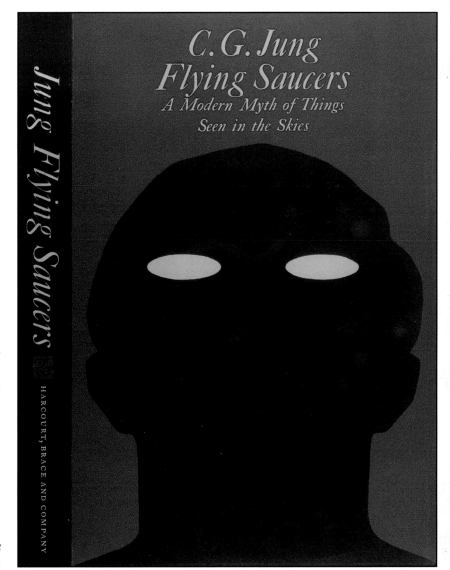

Cover artwork for Carl Gustav Jung's 1958 perceptive study of the UFO phenomenon, Flying Saucers: A Modern Myth of Things Seen in the Skies.

To him as a psychologist, this was an important clue, because he knew from his psychiatric work that it is precisely in people of this kind that the subconscious has to resort to particularly drastic measures, if it wishes its contents to be perceived by the *conscious* mind. The most effective way in which it does this is by projection. The individual externalizes his inner preoccupation as an object outside himself. The flying saucer is the outward representation of the subconscious hope or fear, chosen because it symbolizes the benefits or the menace presented by the otherworldly visitors.

At the time Jung wrote, people had only just started to claim contact with aliens from space, or even that they had been abducted by such aliens. The only contactee case known to Jung was that of Californian factory-worker Orfeo

Angelucci, who claimed to have been chosen by beings from another world as their evangelist on Earth. This case he found of the deepest interest: "without having the faintest inkling of psychology, Angelucci has described in the greatest detail the mystic experience associated with a UFO vision." Angelucci's fairy-tale encounter was, for Jung, a perfect example of myth perceived as reality.

To Jung, whether the encounter experience had any physical reality or not was only of secondary interest. The primary question was to discover what, in the course of the experience, was released from the individual subconscious. The question of whether flying saucers existed was essentially irrelevant to the encounter phenomenon, because encounter experiences occur on a different level of reality to UFO sightings.

# BALL OF LIGHT PHENOMENA

A curious episode of World War Two, which has never been resolved satisfactorily, is that of the so-called "Foo Fighters". These were enigmatic aerial objects that were observed by pilots on both sides, in both the European and Pacific theatres of war. In appearance they were no more than balls of light (BOL), comparable to other BOL phenomena such as feux follets, St Elmo's Fire and ball lightning. But the Foo Fighters were paradoxical both in their behaviour and in the circumstances of their manifestation. For example, on December 22, 1944, an American bomber crew over Germany saw two very bright lights climb towards them from the ground. On reaching the plane, they levelled off and stayed on the plane's tail for about two minutes.

They were huge, bright and orange-coloured, and they seemed to be under perfect control.

During a mission over Austria and Yugoslavia in the winter of 1944, USAF bomber pilot William Leet reported a BOL which suddenly appeared alongside his plane "like a light switch being turned on". He estimated that its distance from the wing-tip was approximately 75 to 100 metres (250–330 ft), laterally, and about 5 metres (16 ft) to the rear. It seemed two- rather than three-dimensional, like the amber light of a traffic signal, but not like any earthly light. Its estimated diameter was 3 metres (10 ft). It stayed with the plane for about 45–50 minutes, then suddenly was gone. It was seen by all the crew:

Our gunners wanted to shoot it down, but I ordered them not to. I told them if it was hostile, it would already have shot us down. Let's try to figure out what it is, I told them.

A duration of more than 45 minutes far exceeds the life-span of ball lightning or any other scientifically accepted BOL phenomenon. Leet himself, in his 1979 book, was sufficiently influenced by UFO thinking to ask "Could it possibly have been a space craft piloted by advanced beings from another world?". He theorized that perhaps the BOL could have somehow protected his plane from enemy attack. However, he does not propose this suggestion with any conviction, and really it does no more than express his bafflement at the experience.

The explanation that comes immediately to mind is that it might have been a plasma created by the aircraft's progress through the atmosphere. If so, it is curious that only one wing-tip created such a plasma, and it is hard to account both for its extended duration and for its intense luminosity in the night sky – there was

*Spacecraft from another world? An alleged photograph of "Foo Fighters" photographed over the Pacific during World War Two.*

*An American B-24 "Liberator" encounters FooFighters during a daylight bombing raid over Germany.*
*Initially these phenomena were believed to be secret weapons.*

nothing for it to reflect from. It was bright enough for Leet and his crew to suppose their plane had been picked up by German searchlights. But they saw no beams coming from the ground, one crew member reported "a blinding glare that seemed to come from above", and more than one spoke of intense heat, which may or may not have been associated with the BOL.

This is just one instance of several such reports which came mainly from the European theatre of war, but also from the Japanese. The most puzzling feature of the Foo-Fighter phenomenon however is that it was mostly limited to a very brief historical period – two or three years of World War Two – and even then occurred only occasionally, in the course of operations in the German and Pacific airspaces. Because the historical context is so clearly a determining parameter, we are constrained to look

to the historical circumstances for an explanation. I think it is legitimate to speculate that some kind of artifact, generated by military activities or associated hardware, was interacting with natural factors to produce the phenomenon.

Dr Richard Haines, in his important study of reports made by pilots during the Korean war, includes many BOL-type observations. Here is one of them:

February 10, 1952: Lieut. Perez, flying a B-29 bomber, reported a globe-shaped object, estimated size 1 metre (3 feet) across ... [its] color resembled the sun, a light orange, occasionally changing to bluish ... the outer edge appeared to be fuzzy and it seemed to have an internal churning movement like flames or fiery gases ... it came in on the same level as the B-29, remained in the same relative position for approx. one minute, then receded on the same path, fading in the distance ...

If the "Foo Fighter" is a naturally occurring phenomenon related to mechanical flight, why does it not occur more frequently? There are occasional references to similar phenomena in a non-military context, such as the following incident which took place on April 23, 1964. The crew of an aircraft flying over Bedford, England, reported a loud bang and a whitish-blue flash of light. A ball of blue light the size of a football appeared on the starboard wing tip. It vanished in two seconds.

The great majority of accounts – particularly those in which a long duration is cited – relate to military flying. We have to ask, are there any special features of military flying which distinguish it from civilian flying? The 2-second duration of the incident just cited falls a long way short of Leet's 45 or more minutes. Can we be sure that we are confronted by the same phenomenon in both cases? Then again,

*During the Korean War the crew of a United States Air Force B-29 bomber reported a UFO over Wonsan, Korea.*

while military aircraft are different in many respects from civil aircraft, they are surely not so very different? The wartime air crews are liable to be in a state of unnatural tension, but there are many circumstances in civilian flying which would also lead to unusual stress and provoke the same psycho-physiological responses. Yet they do not seem to trigger the same BOL reports.

It seems beyond doubt that the Foo-Fighter phenomenon is a real one, in the sense that it comprises a number of observations that are more-or-less similar to one another and more-or-less distinct in some respects from other comparable phenomena. But we cannot be sure how many of the recorded details were accurate, and which were the result of over-interpretation by witnesses in a tense psychological situation. As they are told to us, the objects seem to have manifested more

intelligent control than we would expect from a purely natural phenomenon, but we may be reading more into their behaviour than is warranted. The Foo Fighters remain an intriguing phenomenon, but they do not strongly support the theory of atmospheric creatures.

## PIEDMONT, YAKIMA AND HESSDALEN

At first sight, the phenomena experienced at the three locations mentioned above are unexciting. Even when photographs from BOL incidents at these places are enlarged, they show points of light that could be

stars or aircraft lights rather than some unusual or ominous natural or supernatural phenomenon. At the same time, they are evidently *something*, because there are many hundreds of photographs as evidence.

Equally, it is by no means certain that the phenomena at Piedmont, Missouri, are related to those at Yakima, in Washington State, or that either are linked to those at Hessdalen in Norway. But all three have in common one extremely important feature – each involves low-level BOLs observed within a relatively limited region over an extended period of time. This makes them almost unique. The vast majority of UFOs and other anomalous aerial phenomena occur spontaneously. A witness happens to see them, then reports the sighting to the authorities, the media or to a research organization. Any investigation that is carried out is done after the event – often a long while after – and most often there is no evidence whatever, beyond the testimony of the witness, that anything happened at all. The original description is typically the only material the investigators have to work on.

At these three locations, on the other hand, because the phenomena have been recurrent, the investigators were able to observe them at first hand. Moreover, the observers were not random members of the public, but persons with some degree of knowledge and experience, and in some cases scientific qualifications. In other words, people who were mentally prepared to see the BOLs rather than being taken by surprise, and who were frequently armed with cameras and other appropriate scientific equipment. Consequently, the phenomena have been observed on instrumental recorders. There are many hundreds of photographs, which constitute our best objective evidence for the existence of a BOL phenomenon unrecognized by current science.

They are, therefore, the most comprehensively studied of all UFO sightings. It is of special significance therefore to note that in all three cases – but particularly at Piedmont and Hessdalen – there were indications of intelligent behaviour on the part of the phenomena.

At Yakima, the observations were made in a largely forested area that requires continuous surveillance against the danger of fire. This meant that there were observation posts manned 24 hours of the day and night, located at particularly strategic sites – as well-placed for observing UFOs as fires! Experienced observers, the people here were able to discount the usual natural phenomena, so when they reported things they considered to be anomalous, they had every right to a serious hearing.

Some reports say structured objects were seen, but most sightings – and all the available photos – show only BOLs. Nevertheless, one 1972 witness described an object the size of a two-floor house, and one reported that the object she saw responded to her flashlight. A farmer who saw one of the same lights reported that it affected

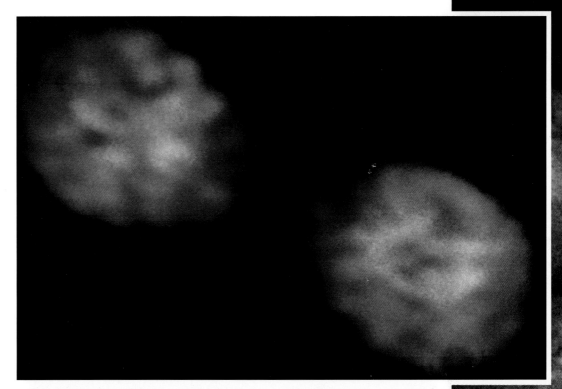

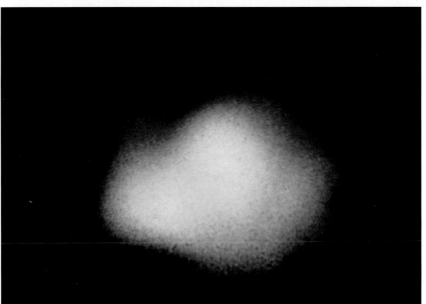

*Ball of Light phenomena photographed in the sky above the remote valley of Hessdalen in central Norway between 1981 and 1984.*

the instruments on his tractor when it passed overhead. So it went on …

Unfortunately, though we know more about these three sets of lights than we do about any other kind of BOL except ball lightning itself, that is not saying very much. In the 1984 series of observations at Hessdalen, for example, though 188 observations were recorded, only two of them were made in conditions that left no reasonable room for doubt that an anomalous event had occurred.

At Piedmont, Missouri, lights were observed in nearby hills and were investigated by physics professor Dr Harley Rutledge over a seven year period. By 1981, when he published his findings, the project had recorded 178 anomalous objects on 157 occasions, under circumstances that seem to rule out either natural phenomena or man-made artifacts. By using triangulation methods based on simultaneous observation from separate posts, the investigators were able to determine the course, distance, speed and movements of the objects. They could consequently eliminate all obvious explanations such as aircraft, satellites, meteorites, car headlamps, street lights, refraction effects, mirages and so forth.

What is of particular interest is that on at least 32 recorded occasions, Dr Rutledge and/or his colleagues recorded a high degree of synchronicity between the movement of the object and the activity of the observers. This activity was sometimes as physical as switching a car lamp on or off, was sometimes a verbal or a radio message, or even an unspoken thought in the mind of one of the observers. There is no way of substantiating this third category, of course. Nevertheless, if we accept the investigators' words in other respects, we must at least give them a hearing

in regard to these remarkable claims.

Of these three sets of phenomena, those most thoroughly observed and documented have been the ones in the remote valley of Hessdalen, in central Norway. From this sparsely populated area have come, since 1981, reports of luminous objects in the sky whose physical existence has been confirmed by more than 500 photographs, along with other instrumental recordings and hundreds of visual sightings.

Although Project Hessdalen has been studying the phenomenon for more than 15 years, with the co-operation of scientists from Japan, Russia, America and elsewhere, no satisfactory explanation is yet forthcoming. The lights often seem to be a metre (3 ft) or more in diameter, can be observed for more than half an hour

RIGHT: *Charles Victor Miller, the American medium who held dramatic seances in Paris. This image shows the materialization of a figure during a seance in 1908 (see p. 45).*

at a time, and have been seen to travel over distances of 20 km (12 miles). Some have been photographed in front of nearby mountains, establishing their exact location. Some very remarkable behaviour has been observed – when a laser beam was directed towards a periodically-flashing "UFO", the flash period immediately doubled, only to resume its previous flashing pattern when the laser was switched off. When the laser was again directed at it, the flashing doubled again. This occurred a total of eight times out of nine.

Needless to say, there is no phenomenon known to science which

*This flying saucer, snowed in among the homes of Hessdalen village, manifests the residents' conviction that their valley is visited by alien spacecraft.*

behaves in this manner. American UFO researcher J Allen Hynek concluded that this "suggests intelligent behaviour". Indeed, though the automatic quality of the response does not imply that the object was consciously responding, it does imply something more controlled than, say, the reaction of an animal when a torch-beam is directed at it.

The sightings at Yakima, Hessdalen and Piedmont do not, of themselves, prove the existence of "space animals". However, they certainly suggest there are stranger things in the Earth's atmosphere than we normally suppose.

## HELPFUL AND HOSTILE

The BOLs witnessed at Piedmont and Hessdalen may have indicated a response that could be taken as an indication of intelligence, but, it doesn't take very much intelligence to respond

to a stimulus by modifying your flashing rate. However, there have been instances where something more seems to have been involved – indeed, to the level of positive interaction with the human observers.

A disturbing case was reported from the Caucasus Mountains in Eastern Europe in 1978.

Victor Kavunenko was one of party of five climbers camped at around 4000 metres (13,000 ft). During the night, he woke with the feeling that there was a stranger in the tent. Looking out from his sleeping bag, he saw a "bright yellow blob" floating about 1 metre (3 ft) from the ground. The object then disappeared into a fellow climber's sleeping bag. The man screamed in pain. The ball jumped out and circled over the other bags, hiding first in one, then in another:

When it burned a hole in mine, I felt an unbearable pain, as if I were being burned by a welding machine, and blacked out. Regaining consciousness after a while, I saw the same ball which, methodically

observing a pattern that was known to it alone, kept diving into the bags, evoking desperate howls from the victims. This indescribable horror repeated itself many times. When I came back to my senses for the fifth or sixth time, the ball was gone. I could not move my arms or legs and my body was burning as if it had turned into a ball of fire itself. In the hospital, where we were flown by helicopter, seven wounds were discovered on my body. They were worse than burns; pieces of muscle were found to be torn out to the bone. The same happened to three of the others: the fifth was dead, possibly because his bag had been on a rubber mattress, insulating it from the ground. The ball lightning did not touch a single metal object, injuring only people.

Were the observers being fanciful when they detected hostility on the part of the BOL? Possibly, but there are other cases where there can be no question whether the BOLs were motivated.

A remarkable story was told in 1956 by Peggy Hight, who had been prospecting with her husband for uranium three years earlier in the New Mexico desert. Her husband had gone off on a week-long exploration and, during that time, Peggy became very ill, to the point where she felt herself to be on the verge of death.

As she lay there one afternoon wondering what would become of her, a small light appeared in one corner of the cabin. It grew larger, until within a few minutes it had expanded to a large glowing light. The light moved slowly towards her, changing from a solid ball into a geometric wheel consisting of a central axle out of which radiated seven spokes, encircled by an outer rim. It whirled through her body, leaving a wonderfully clean and refreshed sensation, then disappeared. Peggy felt a surge of vitality and well-being. She then got up, and realized that the light had completely restored her health.

Frau Elsa Schmidt-Falk, a German lady, wrote to me describing an experience she had while climbing in the Bavarian Alps in the 1950s. She had accidentally lost her way:

You will understand that this is rather a heavy mountain tour. There is a good way as well up as down, but one must not miss

*Ball lightning photographed during the summer of 1978 by Werner Burger at Sakt Gallenkirch, Vorarlberg, in Austria*

*Captain Kirk, Spock and crew are transported in* Star Trek. *Do the mysterious entities that help and harm transport themselves as balls of light?*

slowly dropped until it touched the floor, then suddenly it expanded into a human form, surrounded by a thin gauze. And this form spoke, gave its name, in a distant voice and like a dream. A conversation then took place with it. I remember a colossal Hindoo, with a diadem and bracelets shining like diamonds. He strode across the platform in great strides and jabbering incomprehensible words … a negress asked the audience to sing a ridiculous song … a little girl danced …

Beliard, like many others who attended Miller's seances, was impressed by the show, but not entirely convinced. Miller, who was never a professional medium, is not known to have continued his demonstrations, and the question of what he was doing remains unresolved. But if they were genuine, then there is an obvious similarity to the German widow's story.

This story seems to draw us into the world of psychic phenomena. Could BOLs be a manifestation or representation of spirits of the dead returning to earth, or of ghosts? But the following incident doesn't seem to fall into either of those categories:

My elderly cook has told me that on many occasions she has awakened suddenly during the night and has seen a round or oval patch of red, or sometimes white, light on the wall of the room, which disappeared after a few minutes, but after each of these appearances a death has occurred, either in her family or among her neighbours. On one occasion the globe of light left the wall, proceeded slowly across the ceiling and descended near her bed to about the level of her eyes. The day following her son died in hospital … One night a girl was sleeping in her room, and they both saw two lights, and two deaths took place among their friends shortly afterwards …

When BOLs start to share attributes with guardian angels, we may despair of finding a scientific explanation. On the face of it, a blob of light on a cook's bedroom wall doesn't have much in common with organisms inhabiting the upper atmosphere of our Earth. All, or some, or none, may be intelligent entities sharing our universe. But all have some kind of existence beyond the reaches of our current knowledge.

it as I did. Having started a little late for the return, and light beginning to fade, all of a sudden I found myself in a really dangerous position. As a matter of fact one year later a young girl fell to death exactly on the spot where I realized myself to be in an almost hopeless position. All of a sudden I noticed a sort of a big ball of light, and this condensed to the shape of a tall, rather Chinese looking gentleman. Extraordinarily I was not a bit frightened, and also not astonished, it all seemed then quite natural to me. The gentleman bowed, spoke a few words, led me a small path to the tourists' way, and disappeared as a ball of light.

Just as it is no ordinary ball of light which heals a sick woman, so it is no ordinary one which guides a strayed climber down a mountain. It is not likely that occult powers maintain mountain-rescue services in case of emergency, so we must suppose that this helper came to the lady because of her need. Various scenarios suggest themselves, but the simplest one is that her subconscious mind sent out a mayday call, to which the BOL/Chinese gentleman responded.

What was this ball of light which turned into a figure? The simplest explanation is that it was the mechanism whereby the entity could transport itself to where it wanted to be, like the shimmering columns of the transporter in the *Star Trek* television series. If so, we must see the BOL not so much as a thing in its own right, but as something else in a transitional phase.

# CHARLES VICTOR MILLER

That this may be the case is supported by many records in occult literature. Remarkable phenomena were produced by the American medium Charles Victor Miller, especially at Paris in 1906, where Octave Beliard described:

The medium Miller made about 30 phantoms appear in succession in front of about 100 people, myself included. They were large and small, of every age and every sex, and often one saw two at a time. The way in which the phantoms arrived was very strange. In the darkness, above the platform where Miller was lying in trance, we saw a vague luminosity floating near the ceiling, pretty much like a lump of cotton wool, about the size of a fist. This

# INDEX

## Picture Credits

# About the Author

Hilary Evans is an acknowledged authority on UFOs, extra-terrestrial experiences and the paranormal. He writes and lectures on anomaly research, psychical research, folklore and myth, and related subjects. He is a member of the Society for Psychical Research, the American Society for Psychical Research; the Society for Scientific Exploration; the Association for the Scientific Study of Anomalous Phenomena and the Folklore Society. He has written books on many aspects of anomaly research, notably *Intrusions*; *Visions, Apparitions and Alien Visitors*; *Gods, Spirits, and Cosmic Guardians*; *Frontiers of Reality*; and *Alternate States of Consciousness*. He is the author of four books on UFOs: *UFOs, the Greatest Mystery*; *The Evidence for UFOs*; *UFOs 1947–1987* and *UFOs 1947–1997* and has published many articles on these subjects. He was also writer–consultant for *Almanac of the Uncanny* and several other Reader's Digest publications. He lives in London.